Things to Say When You Have Nothing to Say

BY

Kerry Trautman

ROADSIDE PRESS

Roadside Press
Meredosia, Illinois

CONTENTS

I

THINGS TO WANT WHEN YOU
DON'T KNOW WHAT YOU WANT

All Roads Lead to The Gasconade River 3

Where Trees Grow.................................4

April 22: Birthday of Charles Mingus and Louise Glück 5

To the Bleak March Highway.................................6

The Sound of Your Own Voice 7

Flightless.................................9

Eulogy for a Living Poet................................. 11

Listening to a Poet in a College Chapel as Autumn Rain Pelts Black
Windows................................. 12

What I Want to Read 14

The Blue Hole 16

Water Line 18

Thinking of You Not-Thinking of Me................................. 19

Experimentalist................................. 20

Anthology with Blue................................. 21

Dream 23

Things We Can't Fix 24

He Hid in the Basement................................. 25

Winter, and I Want................................. 26

Bridges 27

Waitress 29

Two Small Town Girls 30

If I Moved to France 31

To Everyone I Could Have Fucked but Didn't 33

Bolstering 34

Erosion 35

Diagnosis 36

Gravity 37

All 39

Washing 40

Things We Don't Think About 41

Revelry 43

Old West End Festival 44

What I Want 46

Things to Believe in 47

II
THINGS TO SAY WHEN YOU
HAVE NOTHING TO SAY

Gary—St. Martin High, Class of '63 49

Flown Loose 50

Plaid 51

Things We Don't Hear 52

Sense of Smell of Fear 54

Tenant #2 55

Dislocation 56

Advancement 58

Hunkered-Down 59

Black Ink Letter 60

Hangover 61

Forget-me-Not 63

As Yellow 64

Eternity 65

Fort Lauderdale Vacation, January 66

Translations from the English into Admissions of Everyday Fears.. 68

When She Found My Father Dead 69

Sleep 70

Reservoir 71

Imagining Myself Alone 73

How to do Things 74

Things to Say in Quarantine 75

Water Falling 77

Alternatives 78

Packing 79

Hermit Crab 81

Things We Don't Ask About 82

Flinching 84

Morning Phone Calls 85

Stuff 86

When Drinking Alone, the Mind Ponders Unknowable Things .. 87

Chemistry 88

How to Avoid Things 89

Support 90

Hermit Crab II 91

Be Fruitful 92

Publication Notes 94

About the Author 95

I

THINGS TO WANT WHEN YOU
DON'T KNOW WHAT YOU WANT

All Roads Lead to The Gasconade River

Life gifts us with versions of ourselves.

Will you be the braid-tail horse who leaps the fence then shits
on the road leading to freedom?

Most major roads lead to water eventually. You'll spot the
treeline in the distance. Close enough, you'll hear it. Follow the
gurgle and heron.

Some creeks flow every day right across narrow roads which
somehow don't erode. Trust your wheels to splash you right
through.

Will you be the hummingbird lapping sugarwater through a
plastic bloom, or will you risk buzzing away toward liatris and
larkspur on the opposite bank?

When a dead tree limb snaps crack and gives way, falling to the
river it doesn't ask which way is downstream which way up. It
figures it out.

Some hills need 4-wheel drive. Some only need the just-right
touch on the gas, the wheel, the ideal weight of the folks
beside you in the car.

Ask a friend which way to the river, and let them lead you
there, down steep gravel road, through thicket, past a horse
who asks for a quick pat. Give it.

Where Trees Grow

Because of August, bonfire leaf smoke impending, my lips
crave peach fuzz, my chin juices, my teeth, the fibrous flesh near
the pit. So I drove Route 2 east to 269, to Bergman's Orchard,
a place that, in childhood, always meant peaches in the car,
sucking drips between fingers, dribbling on t-shirts, bare knees,
whipping wet pits out the window, wondering if, where they
landed, in a ditch along 269, a tree might grow.

April 22: Birthday of Charles Mingus and Louise Glück

"writing is a kind of revenge against circumstance" —Louise Glück

Days bop along
        atop
       each other

   like ragtag treetops

or like
    highway-side house fence lines—
               one chainlink,
           one grey wood slats or brown,
      leaning leaning leftwise down toward moss—

so what if there's an iris
          here

or   there   a daffodil

    I still slump to the linoleum floor
    in a flea market antiques store

      and moan   aloud

        what were all these iron tools for
         and pie birds and
            beaded evening bags—

afterlives heaped
   on nicked oak tables
     to be combed through

     when it rains out

To the Bleak March Highway

Eyes mesmerized by lines guiding my way here, their ways there, I am suspicious of your gargoyle hawks and lurking turkey vultures. Gasping at black trash bag scraps billowing, before realizing they are not cats. Mourning your too-many wheat-colored, furblown heaps that once were fawns. Eyes aimed beyond your asphalt and time, needing you just now, yes, but relief like lavender ache in joints and eyelids when I've turned free of you to greenish nearly-live lawns, yard-sized birds, a calm neglect of focus.

The Sound of Your Own Voice

How does one Tern or Wren discern a friend's call when I turn
every time I hear *Mom!* called across a crowd?

Each bird's warbling squeaks and chits too similar, whether
Lesser Tit or Greater, whether Pitpit or Plover.

In high school there were girls I wanted to be friends with,
though I didn't know much about them.

A friend tells me I *write about birds a lot.* And I do, though
they're basically strangers.

There are birds I recognize by body or sound, but few I know
by both. I want to befriend them.

If someone calls *Terry or Karen* I will whip my head, searching
for who might need me.

Would I know a Blackbird if it was night? In daylight would I
assume a Meadowlark?

I have one of those faces that looks like other people's. I am
one of those bodies easily forgotten.

Turning my ear toward birdsong doesn't always reveal a body.
A watched beak doesn't always sing on cue.

Who are you, I hear? A Hedge Sparrow, House Sparrow, or, if
it's dusk or night, a Pipistrelle?

A friend says it's ok that I hate the sound of my own voice,
says she hates hers too, says no one really hears theirs right.

Am I to blame for turning toward what I think is my name,
shooting awake having heard it, ears cottoned full of hope?

Flightless

The artist slumps over her sketchpad
             as the crowd stutters   past
watches feet for   pauses
      at her booth
                             A jet engine hides
                                   behind   clouds

                She thinks, he would have known
                        if it was an F16 or Delta
                           Tomcat or Southwest
He used to identify jets
      as they flew overhead
the way
      she spots raptors—
                wingspans   and
                    proportions of bodies
                        giving them away
the flap or soar
 the roar or cry
                overhead focused below
                    toward up-tilted necks
She wonders how
eight different women can
        pass   a painting
see eight different   things
      eight different   reasons
           why or why not   eight
               destinations

Maybe it's all a matter of
               flight patterns
                       of what we leave   behind—
                               exhaust trails   tailing
                                       or tailfeathers
She sketched a feather
                       willed it to   f l y.

Eulogy for a Living Poet

You are so easy to love, and so hard to withstand—your body forever slumped in public bathroom stalls, cracked and coughed with blood wine eyes. Yet, in your laughing moments, you revel, breathe through your pen words we taste for days, words birthed of violins, words for weaving negligees, to remind us you are here still—like grapes which must first be crushed before relinquishing wine.

Listening to a Poet in a College Chapel as Autumn Rain Pelts Black Windows

Undergrads jot notebooks. Purple umbrella puddles rug. A man sneezes, and though I don't see, I know he doesn't cover it.

If a sneeze really spreads a 200-foot radius, did it mist the young man with a handsome red volume of *The Complete Shakespeare* poised on his lap like a trophy wife?

The poet grips the podium with his left hand, book with his right.

A few pews up a man eats Chinese food from a white carton— its flaps wide to the vaulted ceiling. His eyes lock on the poet, chopsticks hoisting peapod to saucy lips.

An old man squints to hear better. A young woman stares limp at the poet—a little in love.

The food must be cold from his walk, below umbrella, clenching his hood against wind. If rain falls 20 miles per hour, how many drops struck his umbrella en route to the chapel?

Someone stifles a sneeze in a snorty plug that throbs my eardrums in sympathy. If a sneeze bursts 100 miles per hour, can the person still hear?

Slick noodles droop across chopsticks like Rapunzel's locks, or a waterfall drawn upward to its source. Are they Szechuan—flecked with red chilis—or syrupy with teriyaki?

The poet leans, inadvertently brushing lower lip to mic.

If a serving of Kung Pao shrimp has 1000 milligrams of sodium, when will the man begin to bloat like a rain-soaked book?

Words settle on our shoulders like sunbeams or snow.

From the rain we all came, and to the rain we shall return, when finished nourishing ourselves with this particular listening.

Are we damp with each other's saliva droplets in chapel air as well as words and rain, and if so do we mind?

What I Want to Read

I heard:
> write the poems you want to read

but I don't know what I want to read
>> until
>>> it spills
>>>> over me
>>> like being caught in a rainstorm

I want words   exuded
>> into the room
>>> like silver-streamed fumes
>>>> from an incense burner

words dragged
  to the river's surface
    flapping   like   a
>>> snagged   carp

words panned-for
sifted
arisen in
a glinting gift
from silty nothings

I don't want to read the poems I would write

I'd rather choke
> on words from someone else's throat
>> like second-hand smoke

the way a chicken
                tastes better
        when roasted in someone else's kitchen

With   nothing
                    to give
                            I   wait

for something
            to be   given

The Blue Hole

The pits of his eyes only reflected my face like staring into the
Blue Hole roadside attraction as a kid—highway billboards
proclaiming the pond a bottomless Mystery.

Did he ever even unpack his boxes—knowing in two years he'd
leave again, and in two years again? Grad school, PhD, poet-
in-residence, strings of different states, offices, Student Union
buildings, coffee shops to laptop in, colleagues and students
expecting to be impressed.

The Blue Hole's chemistry—its magnesia, and lime, iron and
soda—keeps green things from growing. Fish can't live, even
if the water wanted them, wanted its perimeter—small enough
a boy could toss a football across—to be ringed with anglers
dangling what they brought to wriggle and tempt a bit of
scaled life through the water's surface to their hands.

Maybe unpack, but not break the boxes down—nest them in a
closet, like an illness in remission.

Or maybe break down, but slide in a flattened stack below his
bed—princess without that pea to trick her to admit her back
is broken.

How to crack your traumas open to strangers, hoping for a
friend, when you'll soon haul yourself away? How to care
about someone who can never be your home?

The Blue Hole is fed by an unseen underground stream, water temp 48 degrees—constant regardless of August drought or February frost, despite flood or water-main breaks, widening highways or ocean rise.

I know his books, but not his throat voice, his poems but not his mind. I want to watch his eyes in pure dark, where my own reflection can't encroach, want to see to the bottom, where a boy child sleeps curled in a nest of sand.

As a child I tossed a penny in the blue water, leaning, listening for a plink of hitting bottom that never sounded. As if that one blink of sound would be enough for me to calculate the mystery of depth.

Now here with us, to teach in our city, he is home, for as long as he chooses to stay. How do we teach him how roots work? Not just hydroponics, or the restricted volume of a terracotta pot, but a chosen plot of bottomless earth.

Water Line

I was thinking how you never took me fishing, and everyone says how peaceful, and they have these revelations like not getting over Aunt Pam's death, or the garage could be a rumpus room if we add berber and fluorescents, and a bar along the back, and plumbing run down through the kitchen wall, and I was thinking maybe with a walleye hooked red in the mouth, tugging at my Erie-Dearie, my line of thought would lead for once to anywhere other than that place where your upper lip slides wet against your bicuspids.

Thinking of You Not-Thinking of Me

You're probably on a plaid couch, blue-tv-light splashed in your eyes, beer in hand, or maybe a notebook and pen. Probably on the phone with a girl who wears spandex for you and phone-sex whispers just to hear your grin. You're maybe standing, unaware of the bend of your elbow, tilt of hip. Maybe sleeping, dreaming of summiting evergreen mountains, not worrying I'm scared of heights, or dreaming of fist-fighting some guy who cut you off on the highway, not remembering what kind of car I drive. Filling the smaller hours of your night with visions of anything but my laugh, or my hair and how it shimmers auburn in full sun.

Experimentalist

He used *in the sack* in a poem, and he meant it.

There should be a saltshaker in every garden to sprinkle warm, yanked tomatoes.

I watch the orange wedge make a home for itself between his lips and teeth, pulp to his gums, sweet.

He writes erotic poetry like salting his eggs—without first tasting.

His voice itself reminds my nose of freesia, my shoulders of sunlight, my toes of low tide, my tongue of August pears, my stomach of warm milk, my eyelids of half-moons, of wine.

Every time I buy a grocery tomato, it refuses to taste like July—disappointing like an over-dry kiss, a sunset with no red at all.

His poems are fluorescent light—blue distortion of color.

I want to swallow the last swallow of warmed red wine in his glass, because of what lingers there besides wine.

I tried a yellow cherry once. It didn't taste like a red one, but it was good anyway.

Anthology with Blue

Choosing a blue paint for
                        the front door
samples taped in changing light
        glass muting what the sun tries

Secure Blue
Honorable Blue

Last night I dreamed the name
                        Ray   McNiece
realizing only this morning when
        I spotted the name jotted near notes from
                last month's conference

Dynamic Blue
Major Blue

His name   and   the name of an anthology
                                of Detroit poems
inked in the margin of drafted
        lines of a   fairy tale   I haven't written

I think he's from Cleveland

Rhythmic Blue
Celestial Blue

I did not dream the perfect   blue
                nor

the Lake Erie shore
                nor
his poem I think
            I read in an anthology
            of Cleveland poems
                        gifted from a new poet friend with
                        brown eyes like cherry cordials

Pulsating Blue
Wondrous Blue

Dream

In the meeting he's busy watching that intern and that place
where her hairline teases the back of her neck with little curlies,
and he remembers—he doesn't know why—that he's due for an
oil change, and maybe after work tomorrow and before the stop
at the recycling center, and damn does he ever wish he could roll
over after that dream about the tunnel and the whale with yellow
teeth, and while he's sweating, panting, roll over and mush his
face in that neck of hers and sniff and sleep again.

Things We Can't Fix

I trust that every empty room is holding its breath, waiting to allow the next warm person inside. *Have a seat. Stay.*

My interior is displayed like a jeweler's case—locked and twinkling, blocked from close inspection, artificial light.

Stars puncture darknight in hopeful slivers with nothing to reflect off.

Broken mechanisms won't always interlock, after all. Their gears end up in a rusted coffee can on a workbench, or in a scrap heap—recycled, crunched.

Time clinks itself inside my skull, unknowing its *tick-tick-tick*s are mis-calibrated.

Manhattan hotel rooms are lonely between check-out and check-in. But those in small towns expect emptiness for days on end. It's all about how to absorb vacancy.

By the time we see a star's light, it has likely been dead for years.

There are no keys jangling on a handyman's hip. No keys at all.

He Hid in the Basement...

throwing things away to save space, but space is for saving things,
filling the rooms you live in with reminders of what you've loved
about life—playbills with your friend's name highlighted yellow,
outgrown hand-knit sweaters, 45s, dried carnation corsages,
heaps of unlabeled photos, the clipped obituary of your
sophomore-year French teacher, concert wristbands, and the
Kit-Kat wrapper where she first gave you her phone number.
He went upstairs for more trash bags, joy in his voice—joy for
the empty growing of empty space down empty where he was.

Winter, and I Want (after "Dress Impression with Train,"
glass sculpture by Karen LaMonte)

Winter   and I want to strip   slip into the glass gown
          be a ghost of a woman   still   translucent

                    chilled   with a slumped lilt of shoulder
                                                  downward   left

ice dress   ice gallery

desperately sunlit windows behind
          and beyond them century-old houses
                    wide porches icicled like yeti's grins

my cloth draped as Artemis spotting hawks—
          still   and dark
                              like gingerbread against frosted branches
                                        and layers of
                                  snow   and   snow

ice gown   ice room

I want to crave the handblown fire of the hot-shop men
          blowing red slag to billowing life beyond
                    their cooled insulating windows

ice robe   ice walls   iced body

                                        born of heat

Bridges

My brother moved to San Francisco with a working fear of bridges.

I'm not afraid to burn bridges that make kindling of themselves.

San Francisco has 23 miles of bridges.

Sometimes the things we're afraid of hang themselves from steel cables.

I've never burnt a bridge I regretted burning.

Five died building Toledo's Glass City Skyway bridge, and another killed himself with it.

My friend Donora wrote a book of poems called Jeff Bridges. Each poem is titled Jeff Bridges.

We tourists gathered on the Tower Bridge in London, all singing the song inside, imagining ways of falling down.

Only 26 people survived jumps from The Golden Gate Bridge. 1,700 instead succeeded.

Sometimes people cross from one side to another. Sometimes people cross one another.

My friend Michelle moved to Florida with a working fear of bridges.

Grandpa still made caramel-corn after his bridge, but he never ate it, but he watched us eat it.

Florida has over 9,000 bridges.

My dad followed the bridge game printed in the Sunday paper, crossing-out things, I don't understand why.

258 Floridians have leapt from the Sunshine Skyway Bridge.

Bridges can double themselves above still water.

People can lose themselves into still water.

Sometimes we watch people cross things out without understanding why.

Waitress

A poet cannot live on eggs alone, searching for inspiration in burnt bacon and coffee-stained tabletops, hoping someone might babble wisdom into their Denver omelet for her, hoping to catch a useful aphorism from the walking-through-the-dining-room bits of rumbled chatter. And along towards the time where she begins to hope the dishman who mutters Fleetwood Mac to the pancake and hashbrown scraps as he scrapes from platter to trash might indeed lead a secret life of vigilante crime, she decides it's time to get out.

Two Small Town Girls

They walked along the storefronts—several boarded-shut, or emptied to dingy linoleum, labeled *for sale,* since a two-years-ago flood. They peered in the antique store and the bridal boutique with a single hopeful shopper fingering the satins, and they wished to slip into those voluminous, shimmery gowns, or lie on the lavender velvet sofa in the thrift store window, or lap the garlicky sauce wafting its warmth from the door of the diner as a man shambled out, full, unsmiling. They ticked their quick feet down the rigid sidewalk, a dry unsettled wind whipping leafy debris against brick walls, sandstone, cinderblock—the trash of the weeks twitching as it landed in cold corners, or stuck between curbs and parked tires, or hurled upward toward the frayed canvas awnings, toward upper apartment windows, toward the networks of suspended iron stairs no one ever has used for escape.

If I Moved to France

I wouldn't be able
     to say what I see in the clouds

    Les nuages.

I could say *blanc*
        white

but not describe
    a white that changes whiteness
      with the wind and height
        of the sun in

              le ceil

            sky

white against *bleu*
       blue sky

      haut

      up high

I could be right to say

       blanc et bleu

except when the clouds aren't white
    except when the sky isn't blue

I couldn't name animal shapes there
or wonder about rain

la pluie

couldn't explain
not to trust

le ciel
ou les nuages

couldn't speak of
fear or wishes

To Everyone I Could Have Fucked but Didn't

I used to suck every popsicle I wanted, sip all the pop I could
tickle my throat with, so why didn't I open the door for every
knock—be like Sandy trading poodle skirts for black leather
painted-on pants?

What if I had unclasped my bra, placed your hot palms under
the hem of my shirt, guided you to slide them up up?

What if I had taught your mouth how to feed itself, leaned
into your fingers' reach when my skin was at its smoothest, or
straddled your laps in theater seats, film light flicking the back
of my hair?

What I wanted was your mouths, the meat of your asscheeks in
both my hands, your pectorals weighing me down.

What if I took what I wanted—pressed my cheek to the pulse
of your stomach, tasted every flavor that smelled good, wore
every color I thought looked right on me?

What if I let you at my button fly, locked eyes as you one-
two-three-four opened and cupped the wet heat you were
after? What if I owned my desire instead of wasting, wanting,
waiting?

Bolstering

She feels uglier as of late—starting to sag skin over her waistbands, acne still at age thirty, fat pads swelling above her kneecaps when she pulls shorts on her white legs the first warm April day. So she makes herself remember an ex-lover—the one with brown backskin like vinyl, and one dense black eyebrow awning over both black eyes, and an ass like January clementines. She remembers how he always kept the lights on. How he took her left foot into his mouth, grinned around the toes, told her she tasted of pinot grigio and smelled of newborn kittens. She can still feel the warmth around her toes, the cool shock air when he slid them out.

Erosion

She stumbles to the cornfield due for plowing under, crackling
brown under sandaled feet with chilled toes, under woolish night
with mothhole stars, her body raw beside dry stalks, why, she
thinks, why does every surface her skin touches, every fingertip
reaching for her armskin in the dark of a velvet movie theater or
palm on her lower back in a crowded club spark and rub her raw.
Thinking how sad the corn's been grown and given-up and still
there's some left that got missed, she figures this must be how
the pebbles in a stream feel.

Diagnosis

I am a vinyl-chrome-marble-mirror hotel lobby—reflective
rather than plush.

No, I am not, but I armor the floral compost of my body
practically—the way hoteliers appreciate impermanence, the
ease of wiping memory of skin from plasticized hide.

What sort of *-itis* is this that I have? Who wouldn't want to
be wrapped in another's body like a sleeping bag on the forest
floor with crickets and Orion's belt, unwound, dropped to the
ground? Or sitting, sangria-drunk, on a Lake Erie sandbar,
water lapping your ribs, ass sunk in sand?

I suppose it's some genetic disease, or calcified nerve endings.

Vinyl has its uses, but so do silk, velour, ostrich leather.

What pill can I swallow with black coffee in my 7am kitchen to
melt linoleum to a bearskin rug with wide eyes, to move in to
my body permanently, un-tape the boxes, let anyone stay?

Gravity

I try to
        direct my eyes   s k y w a r d

my lines taking new
                forms
                like imagining strings connecting
                                star   to   star

                        to create   Ursa   or   Diana

Accustomed instead to tracing
asphalt cracks
bricked pathways
footfall   by   footfall

But I cannot seem to
                covet make-believe
with so much
concrete underfoot

such satisfying gravity

Why pretend
        stars are anything other than
        distinctive bodies of bright heat?

Every time I think my neck

               knows how to lift my brain

          to something up

                up there

it gives out

like a tomato grown so large

       it snaps its own stem.

All

It's not that I'm glad you are all away, not that I prefer hearing only rain and the keyboard and my own pink brain and more rain and the sump pump's hum ejecting it all away. But there is, in this wet silver quiet a soaking of myself into myself. A vein-deep calm like post-coital sleep. It's not that I prefer writing alone over the all-ness of you all, but there will be a day, after all, when I or you or all of us are all gone and I need some small sound left of me.

Washing

Two cantaloupes into the kitchen sink, wetted and soaped
them up the way the cook at my first waitressing job showed
me, saying, *Yeah, I know nobody's eating the rinds, but I'm not putting
those dirty things on my clean cutting board.* So into the sink, like my
babies, when stooping over the bathtub, hurt my back, my knees,
cramped with the gentlest firm grip on their lathered skins, so
into the sink instead, with sun through the western window, and
the yard beyond and what grows there.

Things We Don't Think About

It's too hot to think about last-season's wind-fallen seeds that
became this year's insurgence of zinnias.

Sun rays crush foxglove like a ball-peen on anvil.

As of today I remember my July skin, age seven, grass
clippings clinging to sprinkler-wet bare feet.

Sun shrinks potting soil from terra-cotta circumferences
around the petunias in their shriveled purple gowns.

Zinnias will withstand this heat a while longer. Not the irises—
gone for weeks.

The summer I turned nine, drought cracked everyone's yards
in a new city whose streets I didn't know. I bike-rode to the
neighborhood pool with no intention of returning home.

If I snuck into the back yard of my six-year-old skin, I don't
suppose the iris beds would still be there.

Do zinnias with petals orange as wildfire remember having
been seed? Do they feel their red core toughening, its pliable
frocks dissipating, bees hovering off toward roses who will bud
into November?

As of today I remember being seventeen and terrified how
everything leafed outward despite itself.

When a swimming pool is filled-in, does the soil know it
doesn't belong? Does it remember being trucked and dumped,
with a child nearby crying at its arrival?

As of today I remember twenty-seven, three kids, unaware of
two more. A thorn bush can't know how many rosebuds will
bloom.

A rose doesn't know if it's Princess Grace or Tropicana, but it
knows when it goes to hips.

Do zinnias know they held out so long for a reason?

Some day soon I won't be seven anymore, or twenty-seven.
Some say I'll learn not to sunburn.

I'd like to think the zinnias know, that sunflowers whisper
down folktales of future goldfinches seeking seeds with zeal of
youth, fanning heat in tiny flaps of feathered celebration.

A tale of uneaten seeds dropped to soil, invited into cool damp
of autumn, then spring again, again.

Revelry

Too many birdsongs to count, and me on the sunny deck
with an over-icy Diet Coke and a journal whose contents page
contains my name, several others, and Marge Piercy. Today I
wrote four terrible joyous poems, the babies chase each other,
pants smudged sherbet-y with sidewalk chalk, and I have a
sandwich: wheat bread, pastrami, iceberg, mustard, cheese—
three different kinds.

Old West End Festival

competing musics
                    plucked and blown
                                into the breeze of
                            an outdoor art fair

        into street after street of
                yard sales   and   backlawn parties.

Harmonica and bass guitar blues-ing from
                                    front porch   deep shade
acoustic guitar   Stevie Wonder cover
        from an iron gazebo

Bratwurst   weed smoke and rose gardens
                    swirl with the strumming and
                            waft   down   boulevards

Humid cloudcover graciously holding off
                                rainstorms for   later

the bluesmen
            blessing
                walking feet

a cardinal   a bluejay

a joyous   helloooo! shrieked from
                            a moving car   window

the   flick pull flick
of fingertips on strings

      of vocal chords on lungs

         of songs on our
            eardrums   and leg-skin

What I Want

What I want just now—and I want, of course, many things, even while reminding myself of the foolish ingratitude of the act of wanting—but what I want at this moment—bare toes pacing the wooden backyard deck, unread book in one hand, the other patting the restless sick baby at my shoulder, as the sun sets, casting lilac glow on the single low cumulous cloud between two neighbors' houses—what I want, desire thick, coating my mouth's insides—what I want is to be one of the mud-dauber wasps circling their nest on the shaded underside of the deck's wooden bench, leaving their encapsulated coves to hover over blossoms of their choosing, floating upon any breezes that appear, returning, of course, but without others asking what their day has wrought, as long as they've still brought the customary fluids to share.

Things to Believe in

Bleary eyes searching for the lines of the highway, the sky cold, clear with stars, I drove slow home, thinking about those red-eyed things you said to me, things that twist bone, things I knew you'd never say again. Driving, I saw in the sky over a highway-edge field—that thing, that trio of lights swooping. That sky thing I saw once driving slow home with my mother—light tripod gliding like a drunken bat, nocturnal kite—and Mom pulled over, grabbed her camera, muttering, *I know it's not an alien or anything, I just want to watch.* And she did, cars whizzing past, a part of her, maybe, wanting to believe.

II

THINGS TO SAY WHEN YOU
HAVE NOTHING TO SAY

Gary—St. Martin High, Class of '63

Mom showed me Gary's photo in the newspaper—an article about recycling. She looked at it closely and for far too long. Said she hadn't realized he'd moved to Elmwood five years prior. *Fifteen minutes away,* she said, and I saw her thinking: *ten, if you make all the lights.* She pointed, *his beard used to end here,* and her fingernail traced his jawline, lingered at the cheek. The beard was clean and even, unlike my father's mustache—frazzled like frozen tentacles, as if it would scratch if they ever kissed. *One time, Gary said…We were working on yearbook committee, and Gary said I was…* she began, as if unsure of whether to finish, as if the sentence was doomed to be a waste of words.

Flown Loose

My mother released   my body   from her own

like a blanket   blown
        loose from bungee cords
              in the bed
                    of a pickup truck,
                          winging   over   the highway,
stuck for a day
        on pavement under
              rumbles of tire rubber,

a day in a   still   ditch
        with toads and redwing
                    blackbirds,

a day draped
        on a chainlink fence, a flapping cape,

not even the   wind
        knowing   where   or   when

            I'd fly

                  next

                  or why.

Plaid

You look like you don't have a mother, mine would say, frowning at my rumpled plaid school uniform skirt, my wrinkled white-ish blouse. And I understood it to mean I should shake them out good before dressing, should hang them on my closet doorknob after school, should keep them as near to ironed-looking as I could, though the pleats could never crisp themselves, would instead widen with crosshatch yawns like a bored bedspread. She would sigh at me then drag her tote bag to the public school, leaving me to take the Catholic bus. I wore the skirt as many days as possible, until I spilled chocolate milk at lunch, or slid down the slide too fast into its mud-patch terminus, then I tossed it sheepishly into the laundry pile, used skirt number two. Until I taught myself the machine, learned laundry like a mother, knowing it was supposed to be enough that I had been given the plaid at all.

Things We Don't Hear

Given a pelican's worth of feathers, I still couldn't fashion us a quill.

Hold your ear to a glass pressed to the wall and listen.

Every conversation I have with you might as well be spoken into
the mouth of a Black Scoter diving under Lake Erie.

We would scream out if we fell in the lake, wouldn't we?

Given an eBay's worth of HAM radios, I still couldn't tune us in.

Waves and wings won't listen.

Sandpipers stroll past drownings without announcing a thing.

Glass tubes and wire repeat sound without translation.

I win many of our arguments because you don't even know we are
having them.

Given a cupboard's-worth of smashed glasses, I still couldn't
fashion us a lighthouse lens.

Sailors know when to radio shore for help.

When we repeat repeat, we hold our breath and duck under water.

Glass fishing floats from Japan that wash ashore in Georgia can't
say how they got there.

Herons ignore capsizing.

If lighthouses would cast kaleidoscopes offshore, it could be like hope instead of just dry land.

If a bittern taught me Japanese, would I better understand you?

Waves and wings and lighthouse lights repeat repeat and it's meant to be comfort.

Mute Swans can't radio-in a man overboard.

If I cast arms-full of broken glass into Lake Erie, how long before it resurrects on someday sand, tumbled and scuffed so it won't cut?

Given a lake's-worth of floating gulls, I still couldn't learn how not to go under.

Sense of Smell of Fear

I do not hate my mother, I say to my basset hound, as I let the answering-machine pick up. He perks his flop-ears, sniffing the air, wondering how my voice is in two places at once. Sometimes a dog just knows too much.

Tenant #2

If you keep peeling loose edges you might never stop, I warn
myself, patching walls of the old house.

My oldest son has helped some, but not as much as he could.

Layers of painted-over wallpaper, chipped plaster, cheap 1960s
fake wood paneling.

I compose in my head another lecture about applying for jobs.

We patch cracks and gaps smashed or settled open over decades.
My son spackles nail holes, knee- and fist- shaped holes, sands
them smooth.

Why are people so rough on houses he asks.

We can't convince adults how to situate their bodies in their lives.

I sweep away sanding dust, cut-in trim along flooring with an
angled brush. My son rolls on paint, doesn't trust his wrist with
brushwork.

Watch, I say. *You just use plenty of paint, push right up to the edge.*

A train rumbles past. Sweat trickles my temple. He used to be
afraid of train whistles in the distance.

I follow behind him with my brush, straightening his unfinished

Dislocation

We didn't used to
                              hover
            apart

        from each other

and our own selves

but now the ligaments of us
                        refuse a d h e s i o n
like sand dunes

my vertebrae remember
    l e n g t h e n in g
cartilage pockets
for all their give

one   stride   of your legs
always travels
                        further than
three of mine

it's just the physics of your Pyrenees musculature
                versus
            the hillock of me

my tendons remember
        buoyancy

when
you would
lift
all
of
me
up

Advancement

I shouldn't tell you this but, really, last night alone with you didn't mean much more to me than finally taking the plastic sheets off my mattress with confidence, or changing the flat tire by myself, not caring about the I-75 gravel digging pits in my knees, because above all I chose to risk going it alone.

Hunkered-Down

We hunker in the basement—the only place I've ever
hunkered—with a weather radio, flashlight, phone on local
news ap, granola bars, blankets, bottled water, waiting, listening
for that freight train everyone who's survived a tornado swears
they heard.

I wonder should I start hefting stuff upstairs in case power
goes out and the sump pump can't keep us dry.

You went golfing, convinced it would blow over. Because that's
how life's been for you—charmed, just beyond borders of red-
shaded weather map warnings, nothing would dare threaten
your particular roof and bones. And us by proxy, it seems.

I try to mumble *thank you,* playing Uno with our kids on the
basement rug. The youngest crawls in my lap at thunder claps.

These walls and cupboards and all the ways I fortress them
could be stricken like faux-painted foam-board flats after the
last night of a play.

I'm stronger than I look, but there are muscles I would prefer
not being forced to flex.

Black Ink Letter

Sipping a sweet cordial of sunlit August afternoon, rummaging through a drawer full of recipes I'll never try, and contests I'll never enter, I look for a pen that doesn't write in blue, because you hate blue ink. That is one thing that probably hasn't changed. Scratching down meaningless marks to take-up eye-painful empty stationary space, wishing someone had written a book of things to say when you have nothing to say to someone who you no longer know but wish like hell you did, dripping random black ink marks like a golf-course sprinkler splaying spurts of letters and words in circles until nothing of their used-to-be pattern remains in the inky, sprinkler-watery mess, and besides, the landing of the ink is too distant to see it anyways, too far away to really be my words, even if they're finally saying what only black ink can.

Hangover

I miss you so much I almost drank
          my pancake batter

                                   Don't laugh
                                        I miss you,
                                                    really

and I'm tired
              so   tired   because
                          you weren't even there last night
                                      to tell me

                          that's   enough

and my bed was doing that spinning thing

now my head is stomping
                    and lights burn
                                my eyes

                        you know how they get—
                        all puffy-pink

and I miss you
              I wasn't gonna tell you   but—
                                              really

When I woke up and still you were gone
              and my head
            my twirling bed

I made breakfast

You always told me

                    feed a hangover

but while cooking I was crying
    and almost drank the batter
        instead of my coffee—
                              black

                                  remember?

Forget-me-Not

It was fair of you to worry I would forget your birthday.

The crabgrass has overgrown my tomatoes.

Digging in my purse and not finding a pen and paper for new
lines is like hopping out of the car at the grocery and realizing
my purse is at home.

I hear the garden soil calling through the kitchen wall, and I am
off-balance.

My muscles are edgy and weakened from three days without
making a poem.

The neighbor's cucumbers have penetrated the fence between us.

My daughter spins, drops herself to the carpet, says it is hot lava
because she is off-balance.

I remembered I had planted seeds for the Japanese forget-me-
nots only when they bloomed, blue, alongside the coreopsis.

Something's bound to burn when next I fall.

As Yellow

It's sad how we get used to things, she said, straightening the magazines on the coffee table, and I didn't know if she meant the quiet— how it always settled-in after M*A*S*H* and sometimes again after Carson, or if she meant the daffodils she sees from the bedroom window, lining the driveway, and ringing the base of the birches, and how they aren't as yellow now as the year they first bloomed.

Eternity

So I was talking to my friend about constellations, and she leaned in close and told me I smell good, and I said *it's Eternity,* and I suddenly remembered the country apple potpourri Mom used to burn so it would smell like someone was baking with apples, but no one was, and also to hide the ash funk of Dad's Winstons, either from us or from herself, and my friend asked, mad, couldn't I just sit still for one minute and talk something meaningful, and I said *no, I guess not.*

Fort Lauderdale Vacation, January

A group of new friends ambles down a State Park path. We won't be here for long. Birds call from branches. A toddler speaks in Danish. *Someone is there,* the blonde/blue mother translates, *I hear voices in the bush.*

I want to see an iguana, so I turn at every branch crack and rustle. Back in Ohio reptiles aren't so dinosaur-ish. A lyric from *The Last Five Years* runs through my head—in Central Park, near the museum, singing *can we go see the dinosaurs?*

A pair of Blue Jays bickers. We have the same arguments at home. A friend's neighborhood near here is full of peacocks— blocking drives, sunning on roofs.

The next morning I read at a table outside the hotel office. Workers *hello* as they heave trash and unload trucks. A group of old folks meets for taxis to a sightseeing cruise. We move about these unfamiliar places in whichever way suits us, knowing it's temporary.

If I turn my chair toward the rising sun, it will startle the Grey Catbirds chittering in the saw palms. If the blond/blue toddler was here, he would know exactly what they chirp to each other, and he would tell his mother, and maybe she would tell me.

I won't be here much longer. I still haven't seen an iguana up close—just one from our hotel window, slinking the edge of the pool like considering laps.

White folks settled Florida before Ohio. Prehistoric bones
unearthed in both, but no dinosaurs. Birds are older than
dinos, right?

My bones won't be unearthed because I prefer ash, which is
earth, and no one can translate what it has to say. If somehow
I have to remain intact and buried, tuck me in an unmarked
hole, positioned unexpectedly—in an arabesque or crow
pose, maybe add a couple iguanas—so in a thousand years if
someone finds my bones they'll wonder at the meanings.

Or quilt me in Floridian and Ohioan feathers—glossy ibis,
snow goose, pelican, mourning warbler—so no one can know
just what bird I might have been.

Translations from the English into Admissions of Everyday Fears

When she says *See you later,* what she means is: *Sometimes the breeze tries to fray my muscles.*

When she says *I'm tired today,* what she means is: *To cut into an under-ripe cantaloupe is a failure.*

When she says *Pick up some milk on the way home, will you?* what she means is: *My shoes feel like they're from my childhood closet.*

When she says *The mail is late,* what she means is: *If only the baby bunnies never had to fear dogs.*

When she says *Hold me,* what she means is: *or else I might dissipate like smoke.*

When she says *Look! A heron,* what she means is: *Some day, everyone will leave.*

When She Found My Father Dead

she told me   not to come
                              really.

Wake the kids for the bus.

No need to come
                      really.

Aunt Linda was coming.

Not   having   gone
gulps the air in me sometimes

        the way opening
            opposite-side-of-the-house windows
                sucks all the doors shut.

There will always be
        more sleep
        more busses
        more work phone calls to
            cancel cancel-able things

but never another
        hanging-up of phone
        pulling on of pants
        turning over of the engine

            going

                there.

Sleep

I am awakened by moans alongside me in bed—his throat, lungs, resonating deep belly groans that could be his heart giving out—his brain trying to wake him, me, anyone for help, or just as easily he could be dreaming—running from some caped villain, bleeding, lamenting our son's death or mine, fear ejected through his chest, reverberating our walls. Or possibly he's dreaming of lovers—younger, longer legs, more wide, and his pleasure simply sounds to me like sorrow—I lie awake listening to his moon-shadowed groans, wondering where my own moans come from.

Reservoir

This is drinking water, right? my son asks, watching wave-lets
swish the boulders' seaweed tutus.

Yes, I say, not knowing how it works. Not knowing how much
of anything works.

A mower cuts the high grassy incline holding all this water in,
its blade apparatus angled along the steep slope, its cab with
head-phoned driver inside remaining plumb.

So many machines and systems engineered for real purpose.

Then there's me, sitting on a rock trucked-in to create a fake
lake's berm. I wouldn't know how to fish here if we were
starved.

Could I save us both if we fell in?

I can only write about cloudcover obscuring sun that aches
to glint off water. I can sit here and conjure worthless words
while my son wonders how long his phone might last if tossed
in.

He answers his own questions better than I could.

If an earthquake split this miles-around wall that never should
have been here, how far into town would the waters keep
swallowing?

How much of this could we drink?

Sometimes what looks like a lake is just a construction, not
ancient at all.

Sometimes a woman is incapable of being anything more than
a scratcher-down of words, symbols, glyphs.

It would be too easy to tumble off this cliff.

Imagining Myself Alone

He calls it, *a new poem dealing with old stuff,* and I know it will be
another about his wife, five-years dead. I imagine myself alone,
wandering in rainstorms just to feel heavy with wet clothes, as
if the pressure of hands, the weight of down comforters on
cold November Sunday mornings. Myself alone, drinking wine
on the front porch—Merlot because you liked it—listening for
bicycles, thunder. Alone, tearing up my poems as fast as I write
them, leaving the pieces in the wastebasket for weeks, retrieving
them, fitting them together with scotch tape, reciting them to
the bedroom walls to pretend to remember what passion sounds
like resonating on plaster and paint.

How to do Things

          I'm not trying to tell you
how to do things
               my leaving   o p e n   of the front door
               behind me
                   is in no way
                        an invitation to follow
That sand dollar washed up by our toes on Sanibel Island and you
                   quick bent down
                   and grabbed it
                     wiped it
a c r o s s   y o u r   s k y   b l u e   T s h i r t
              and I had hardly even seen it yet
But   today   is not like that
      today   is clouded   right?
              with ordinary pairs of robins swirling on grass
      today   there's not that pair of
                 red jet skis
                     d r i f t i n g
                        eastward
        is there?

Things to Say in Quarantine

We argue the politics on TV—the paper-shuffling sound bites
like a slipcover slid over a cat-scratched plaid sofa.

Could the remote control click me views into other living
rooms, and do wives there finish sentences without repeated
shouts like linguistic backs of hands? Do husbands there listen,
nod, *I see your point?*

I want to hold the volume-down button and see TV graph
lines dip downward in a breath of relief like a bicycle coasting
with legs yawned wide away from pedals.

I avoid you, avoid the suit behind the crested podium like the
oak tree at the park with a two-foot hornet's nest.

There must be characters somewhere who are better scripted.
Someone is getting this right.

I need clairvoyance like a glow-in-the-dark telephone I can lift
to hear my neighbors cleaning their garage with harmonious
chatter, or my two poet-couple friends versing on twin manual
typewriters beside billowing curtains, or the young couple
marrying in the stone church downtown with only the priest
and their parents six-feet apart in the pews.

I need a TV channel to tell me who will live to feel the heat of
summer, and who will have to trust their memory of waves
pulling wet sand around their toes in a fever dream while
blinking their last blinks.

If I turn the TV off I am an ostrich. On mute I could listen
instead to Debussy or Dylan but maps would still glow there—
reddening circles radiating from major cities, sprawling by the
hour.

There must be something to press to my ear.

I'm willing to hear all I've done wrong and what could have
switched it right, willing to beg forgiveness and burn bridges
before I flush red and burst on a map of Ohio, but first I need
to shout into something built to receive my voice.

Water Falling

On the river's rocky shoreline, crumpling dried leaves in fists, listening to traffic whoosh overhead on the bridge. Up there, glancing down at the black river as I pass it over, I see nothing new. Always the same smattering of ducks diving at what they suspect wriggles below the waterline—no one feeds them dry bread, because the sign says not to. Always the six-foot waterfall spanning the fifty-foot river, either a bare grey trickle or an ominous white gush. On the bridge, I know what I will see through the car window glass, yet I look each time, perhaps hoping to see myself perched amidst the damp stones, myself calling upward to the wheels and steel rolling over, calling to look harder, to gauge what the cascade of falls, with its lodged branches teetering at the crest, with its subtle erosion of rock to pebble, what it might whisper, warn in its steady thrum. Call to the cars—driving 25 because the sign says so—that river and I are not simply things to be bridged over.

Alternatives

Ninety-four degrees, and you are too tiny young for outside,
for lying in the redbud's fluttered shade, for stirring katydids
from the zinnias and basil, for salted watermelon wedges,
nibbled rinds chucked into the shrubs, for drippy fistfuls of
cherry tomatoes. Instead, as the air conditioning drones, I
cradle you, pace our floors and read aloud from Whitman and
Millay. I fork a chunk of cantaloupe to my mouth, still reading
as I chew, you smiling at my lips' movements, me at my actual
words.

Packing

She packs dresses, long enough they won't Marilyn in breeze.
Travel-size sunscreen, books, airplane snacks.

Because she dreads being alone with him, she packs also fear
she'll say something wrong, or that she'll have to hear the same
arguments over and over. Different city, same picked-at scabs

She packs her passport—the foil USAs shine copper and silver
in light. She knows just how to hold it to reflect what she
wants.

She packs an endless stream of small-talk—NPR tidbits, funny
TikToks. *Did you hear about that landslide in LA?*

There's much at stake in the nest they've constructed and fly
away from toward high-rise hotels and art museums. A wrong
word could shimmy it all apart like a Jenga block tower.

She packs fancy underwear, a flask for purse Stoli.

For five days sky is blue, an Uber idles at each corner, and if
his eyes drop dark, she ducks into a gift shop to see *I heart
wherever* T-shirts and shot-glasses.

Her itinerary leaves no time to dredge up the shit of real
lives. Feed his vacation high with cocktails from touristy bars.
Distract him with hotel sex, or a Broadway-show-and-rose-
garden smokescreen, so he'll think he sees good in her.

Google the best local ice cream, free walking tour of film and tv locations. Snap selfies at Niagara Falls, Golden Gate Bridge, Lady Liberty.

Hermit Crab

The slick
pink of me

                    is tucked   away
                     in the dark of
                  someone else's whorls.

Water sluices
               through

enough to sustain,

        bringing with it
                        sand.

I   chose   these   walls

        knowing   full   well

           I   will
                   outgrow   them.

Things We Don't Ask About

In a small museum in Allen County, Ohio is a case of objects
a physician pulled from throats of children—bottle caps, keys,
and oh so many aggies and swirlies. What if they had never
tweezed them free?

Months before my dad died, he began online-buying marbles,
a solar-system's-worth—Jupiter, stardust, Milky Way. He didn't
say why. No one asked.

When my mom was young her father renovated the bathroom,
lugging the clawfoot tub to the yard where she played boat,
poured her marble bag, and down the drain they rolled into a
sidewinder of copper pipe. When she told this story, she did
not mention her mother.

Dad had never mentioned playing marbles. I don't know what
they ever saw in each other, except Mom mentioned falling for
his lead-chest DJ voice. Why don't I know the story of how
they met? All I know was they were in a bar. Shot-glasses of
marbles eventually lined their headboard.

Each visit, Dad would open a softly-clinking velvet pouch of
his newest—cat's eye, steely, dragonfly. Mom rolled her eyes,
and I wondered how many marbles she'd stepped on, kicked
under the couch. What did we think would happen if we asked
him when the mason jars would stop filling, when is enough?

We assume glass is fragile, but these orbs of color outlast
decades of dirtyard flicks and plunks down stormwater grilles.

Bright nomads exposing souls in suspended whorls of gold or
scarlet. What makes us afraid of each other?

We teased Mom how she lost her marbles, and humored Dad
his palms-full of metallic and luster. We didn't ask why now?
Why accumulate jars of trinkets we'll have to find a home for
when what we all know is happening eventually does happen?

Doctors know better than to ask why things are swallowed.
And for every glass bowl of marbles on coffee tables in
magazine photos, I wonder whose mouths they have filled,
whose windpipes they threatened to stifle.

Flinching

my feet wind through my small town

    airspace

        between

            my skin   and   everyone else's

    e l e c t r i f i e d

      I am the violet nucleus of a plasma ball
        suspended in a glass globe

reach out—
     see me jolt
        and spark

           see how you flinch too

There is no *we* in *Ohio*

no *us* in *United States.*

     We wince   we ignite

Morning Phone Calls

A call in the morning means you blew a tire on a pothole or a rusted muffler, or black ice on I-75 slid you away, and I can't help thinking, writing here with your favorite pen, next time it could be your plane, and then how could I continue on changing diapers, folding shirts, dusting bookshelves, waiting for the coffee to drip itself done?

Stuff

Pick-ups and vans parked for blocks to bid on the old lady's
stuff. People filing out her propped-open door, arms piled high
with booty. Her life's accumulation in splintered orange crates
and paper Foodtown bags—*two for $5, three for 10*—tracking dead
grass through her emptied parlor. And at the start of our street,
on a flattened Pepsi carton, someone had scrawled in bright red
marker, *auctsion parking   2 bucks   last house.*

When Drinking Alone, the Mind Ponders Unknowable Things

Which different turn of a ten-year-old's bicycle might have lead
to an entirely different lifelong string of lovers.

The exact proportion of water to sand for castling, not
sprinkling away to nothings, not landsliding to shapeless sludge.

My last words to my father. His to me.

Why a deteriorated rope hangs from a dead tree in the
downtown scraggly cliff edge of the Maumee River. Surely no
tire swing.

Even last-ish words might suffice. There must have been a
phone call. *Hey.* Pause. *Is Mom there?*

Lyrics for a melody stuck replaying staggered bits of itself
behind my eyebrows, beyond cumulonimbus clouds, beneath
the dirt's named strata.

What I do wrong each time I mix an Old Fashioned, each
bartender doing it differently, better than the last, so I keep
letting them, keep going.

Chemistry

My son paces   the living room
    talking with excited hands

                        and   rushed breath
about chemistry class

He describes the experiment—

                        Bunsen burner   flame
                        goggles   carbon—
with the joy of a poet
            savoring   each   new detail.

Grandpa   would have loved
                how you enjoy chemistry
I say
    You know my dad   was
                    a chemistry teacher   right?

My son stops
    stares at me   as if I'd said
    I once was sodium   and now

                        sink like lead.

How did I not know that?
he says
And we   both
            add it to our mental lists of
                        unknowables—things to
light flames under   test
                record   what happens to matter
                    when it changes state

How to Avoid Things

The birthday cake is continually sliced thinner and thinner. No one wants to be responsible for eating that last bit.

They move carefully around each other—saying just enough, reigning themselves in when they sense their pace may have more momentum than they can handle.

It might be nice if you... When you have a second could you maybe...

None of them want to know what would happen if the car sped too tight around a curve and outer tires drifted up off the pavement more than a little.

There are mornings when the first one up feels the barometric pressure between quiet doors and drywall pulse like an aneurysm about to bleed out. They wonder what it would take to pop it—tension eased like careening downhill.

Why don't you ever... Can't you just...

If they hurt each other, they hurt themselves—they chisel a crack in the whole tv screen. Then no one will be able to watch stories all roll by in 4K technicolor, so real they could almost reach out and touch.

Support

Rooting through the garage junk for something to support my
tomato plant overgrown its big pot, too late for cages. I find
two scrolled iron seat backs salvaged from a pair of broken-seat
barstools—one of my many salvages, assuming someday they
could be of use. I mash the metal into soil on two sides of the
pot, flop the branches—heavy with green-gold fruits—over the
fancy new supports they waited too long for, drooping in sun
and storm. The plant only needs so much, still I tread so near
failing it. I mean, it's my heart, really.

Hermit Crab II

My Mom's house is my mom's house now. I haven't lived there in
25 years.

The moon doesn't choose the shadows it casts.

My now house is a nautilus shell the bared guts of my children
can crab into ever.

The tide doesn't choose erosion or what it washes to shore.

A house is not a fact or snowmelt. My house is not a turtle. My
house is the equator.

The tide comes back comes back. Blame it on the moon.

My mom's house is my mom's house now. But then it always was.

My door is wide to gibbous light. Bare yourself, slip inside.

Be Fruitful

The old woman hired four apricot trees planted in the back yard, near the property line, assured by the nursery manager they would, indeed, bear fruit, though not before a decade's-worth of soggy April breezes and lonesome bees had whizzed through, uneventfully. She told herself she didn't mind, enjoyed their virginal blossoms nonetheless, pure white as new bedsheets. Someday, someone would thank her. Someone with baskets full and apron pockets laden with honeyed fruits soft as love and succulent as sex, someone would bite, tilt their face to the blueness of the sunlit sky, gasping within their gut, and bless her unknown name.

Publication Notes

The author thanks the publications in which some of the poems in this book previously appeared:

"Water Line" Fuel (1998.) "Black Ink Letter," "Eternity," "Water Falling," "Imagining Myself Alone," and "As Yellow," Things that Come in Boxes (King Craft Press 2012.) "Be Fruitful" Toledo Poetry Museum blog. "Two Small-Town Girls" Mock Turtle Zine (2013.) "Translations from the English into Admissions of Everyday Fears" Clockwise Cat (2014.) "Flightless" Five2One (2015.) "Winter and I Want" A Rustling and Waking Within (Ohio Poetry Association Press 2016.) "Bridges" Red Fez (2016.) "The Sound of Your Own Voice" Gasconade Review (2018.) "How to do Things" Riverdog (2020.) "When Drinking Alone, the Mind Ponders Unknowable Things" As it Ought to Be (2021) and Unknowable Things Roadside Press (2023.) "Hermit Crab" Cool Rock Repository (2021.) "Flown Loose" Everything in Aspic (2021.) "Experimentalist" The Parliament (2021.) "Waitress" and "Hangover" The Disappointed Housewife (2021.) "April 22: Birthday of Charles Mingus and Louise Glück" Sweet Lit (2021.) "All Roads Lead to the Gasconade River" Gasconade Review (2022.) "Dislocation" Swifts & Slows (2023.) "When She Found My Father Dead" Book of Matches (2023.) "Forget-Me-Not" Midway Journal (2023.) "Revelry" and "Sense of Smell of Fear" River Dog Zine (2023.) "Anthology with Blue" Beach Chair (2024.) "Things We Don't Think About" The Schuylkill Valley Journal (2024.) "Hermit Crab II" Many Nice Donkeys (2024.) "To Everyone I Could Have Fucked But Didn't" Peach Fuzz (2025.) "Things We Can't Fix" Steam Ticket (2025.)

Kerry Trautman is a lifelong Ohioan whose work has appeared in numerous international anthologies and literary journals. She has served as judge or workshop leader for the Northwest region of Ohio's "Poetry Out Loud" competition annually since 2016. In 2024, her one-act play "Mass" received a staged reading as a winner of The Toledo Repertoire Theater's "Toledo Voices" competition. Her books are *Things That Come in Boxes* (King Craft Press 2012,) *To Have Hoped* (Finishing Line Press 2015,) *Artifacts* (NightBallet Press 2017,) *To be Nonchalantly Alive* (Kelsay Books 2020,) *Marilyn: Self-Portrait, Oil on Canvas* (Gutter Snob Books 2022,) *Unknowable Things* (Roadside Press 2022,) and *Irregulars* (Stanchion Books 2023.)